THIS FISHING JOURNAL BELONGS TO

NAME

ADDRESS

PHONE

E-MAIL

ESSENTIAL CONTACTS

NAME

ADDRESS

PHONE

E-MAIL

NOTE

NAME

ADDRESS

PHONE

E-MAIL

NOTE

NAME

ADDRESS

PHONE

E-MAIL

NOTE

TABLE OF CONTENTS

PAGE	LOCATION	NUMBER I CAUGHT
1		
2		
3		
4		
5		
6		
7		
8		
9		
10		
11		
12		
13		
14		
15		
16		
17		
18		
19		
20		
21		
22		
23		
24		

25	
26	
27	
28	
29	
30	
31	
32	
33	
34	
35	
36	
37	
38	
39	
40	
41	
42	
43	
44	
45	
46	
47	
48	
49	
50	

MY FISHING LOG

DATE :   (SUN MON TUE WED THU FRI SAT)

LOCATION :

FISHING WITH :

BAIT AND TOOL USED :

WEATHER :   TEMP :

START TIME :   END TIME :

TOTAL TIME USED :

TYPE OF FISH | NUMBER I CAUGHT

1.   #

2.   #

3.   #

4.   #

5.   #

6.   #

7.   #

8.   #

MY CATCH OF THE DAY WAS

FISHING TRIP SCALE OF AWESOME

FISHING NOTE

FISHING DISCOVERIES

MY FISHING LOG

DATE :   (SUN MON TUE WED THU FRI SAT)

LOCATION :

FISHING WITH :

BAIT AND TOOL USED :

WEATHER :   TEMP :

START TIME :   END TIME :

TOTAL TIME USED :

TYPE OF FISH | NUMBER I CAUGHT

1.   #
2.   #
3.   #
4.   #
5.   #
6.   #
7.   #
8.   #

MY CATCH OF THE DAY WAS

FISHING TRIP SCALE OF AWESOME

FISHING NOTE

FISHING DISCOVERIES

MY FISHING LOG

DATE :   (SUN MON TUE WED THU FRI SAT)

LOCATION :

FISHING WITH :

BAIT AND TOOL USED :

WEATHER :   TEMP :

START TIME :   END TIME :

TOTAL TIME USED :

TYPE OF FISH | NUMBER I CAUGHT

1.   #
2.   #
3.   #
4.   #
5.   #
6.   #
7.   #
8.   #

MY CATCH OF THE DAY WAS

FISHING TRIP SCALE OF AWESOME

FISHING NOTE

FISHING DISCOVERIES

MY FISHING LOG

DATE : (SUN MON TUE WED THU FRI SAT)

LOCATION :

FISHING WITH :

BAIT AND TOOL USED :

WEATHER : TEMP :

START TIME : END TIME :

TOTAL TIME USED :

TYPE OF FISH | NUMBER I CAUGHT

1. #

2. #

3. #

4. #

5. #

6. #

7. #

8. #

MY CATCH OF THE DAY WAS

FISHING TRIP SCALE OF AWESOME

☆ ☆ ☆ ☆ ☆

FISHING NOTE

FISHING DISCOVERIES

MY FISHING LOG

DATE :   (SUN MON TUE WED THU FRI SAT)

LOCATION :

FISHING WITH :

BAIT AND TOOL USED :

WEATHER :   TEMP :

START TIME :   END TIME :

TOTAL TIME USED :

TYPE OF FISH | NUMBER I CAUGHT

1.   #

2.   #

3.   #

4.   #

5.   #

6.   #

7.   #

8.   #

MY CATCH OF THE DAY WAS

FISHING TRIP SCALE OF AWESOME

FISHING NOTE

FISHING DISCOVERIES

MY FISHING LOG

DATE :   (SUN MON TUE WED THU FRI SAT)

LOCATION :

FISHING WITH :

BAIT AND TOOL USED :

WEATHER :   TEMP :

START TIME :   END TIME :

TOTAL TIME USED :

TYPE OF FISH | NUMBER I CAUGHT

1.   #
2.   #
3.   #
4.   #
5.   #
6.   #
7.   #
8.   #

MY CATCH OF THE DAY WAS

FISHING TRIP SCALE OF AWESOME

FISHING NOTE

FISHING DISCOVERIES

MY FISHING LOG

DATE :   (SUN MON TUE WED THU FRI SAT)

LOCATION :

FISHING WITH :

BAIT AND TOOL USED :

WEATHER :   TEMP :

START TIME :   END TIME :

TOTAL TIME USED :

TYPE OF FISH | NUMBER I CAUGHT

1.   #
2.   #
3.   #
4.   #
5.   #
6.   #
7.   #
8.   #

MY CATCH OF THE DAY WAS

FISHING TRIP SCALE OF AWESOME

FISHING NOTE

FISHING DISCOVERIES

MY FISHING LOG

DATE :   (SUN MON TUE WED THU FRI SAT)

LOCATION :

FISHING WITH :

BAIT AND TOOL USED :

WEATHER :   TEMP :

START TIME :   END TIME :

TOTAL TIME USED :

TYPE OF FISH | NUMBER I CAUGHT

1.   #

2.   #

3.   #

4.   #

5.   #

6.   #

7.   #

8.   #

MY CATCH OF THE DAY WAS

FISHING TRIP SCALE OF AWESOME

FISHING NOTE

FISHING DISCOVERIES

MY FISHING LOG

DATE :   (SUN MON TUE WED THU FRI SAT)

LOCATION :

FISHING WITH :

BAIT AND TOOL USED :

WEATHER :   TEMP :

START TIME :   END TIME :

TOTAL TIME USED :

TYPE OF FISH | NUMBER I CAUGHT

1.   #
2.   #
3.   #
4.   #
5.   #
6.   #
7.   #
8.   #

MY CATCH OF THE DAY WAS

FISHING TRIP SCALE OF AWESOME

FISHING NOTE

FISHING DISCOVERIES

MY FISHING LOG

DATE :   (SUN MON TUE WED THU FRI SAT)

LOCATION :

FISHING WITH :

BAIT AND TOOL USED :

WEATHER :   TEMP :

START TIME :   END TIME :

TOTAL TIME USED :

TYPE OF FISH | NUMBER I CAUGHT

1.   #
2.   #
3.   #
4.   #
5.   #
6.   #
7.   #
8.   #

MY CATCH OF THE DAY WAS

FISHING TRIP SCALE OF AWESOME

FISHING NOTE

FISHING DISCOVERIES

MY FISHING LOG

DATE :   (SUN MON TUE WED THU FRI SAT)

LOCATION :

FISHING WITH :

BAIT AND TOOL USED :

WEATHER :   TEMP :

START TIME :   END TIME :

TOTAL TIME USED :

TYPE OF FISH | NUMBER I CAUGHT

1.   #
2.   #
3.   #
4.   #
5.   #
6.   #
7.   #
8.   #

MY CATCH OF THE DAY WAS

FISHING TRIP SCALE OF AWESOME

FISHING NOTE

FISHING DISCOVERIES

MY FISHING LOG

DATE :   (SUN MON TUE WED THU FRI SAT)

LOCATION :

FISHING WITH :

BAIT AND TOOL USED :

WEATHER :   TEMP :

START TIME :   END TIME :

TOTAL TIME USED :

TYPE OF FISH | NUMBER I CAUGHT

1.   #
2.   #
3.   #
4.   #
5.   #
6.   #
7.   #
8.   #

MY CATCH OF THE DAY WAS

FISHING TRIP SCALE OF AWESOME

FISHING NOTE

FISHING DISCOVERIES

MY FISHING LOG

DATE :   (SUN MON TUE WED THU FRI SAT)

LOCATION :

FISHING WITH :

BAIT AND TOOL USED :

WEATHER :   TEMP :

START TIME :   END TIME :

TOTAL TIME USED :

TYPE OF FISH | NUMBER I CAUGHT

1.   #

2.   #

3.   #

4.   #

5.   #

6.   #

7.   #

8.   #

MY CATCH OF THE DAY WAS

FISHING TRIP SCALE OF AWESOME

FISHING NOTE

FISHING DISCOVERIES

MY FISHING LOG

DATE :   (SUN MON TUE WED THU FRI SAT)

LOCATION :

FISHING WITH :

BAIT AND TOOL USED :

WEATHER :   TEMP :

START TIME :   END TIME :

TOTAL TIME USED :

TYPE OF FISH | NUMBER I CAUGHT

1.   #

2.   #

3.   #

4.   #

5.   #

6.   #

7.   #

8.   #

MY CATCH OF THE DAY WAS

FISHING TRIP SCALE OF AWESOME

FISHING NOTE

FISHING DISCOVERIES

MY FISHING LOG

DATE :   (SUN MON TUE WED THU FRI SAT)

LOCATION :

FISHING WITH :

BAIT AND TOOL USED :

WEATHER :   TEMP :

START TIME :   END TIME :

TOTAL TIME USED :

TYPE OF FISH | NUMBER I CAUGHT

1.   #

2.   #

3.   #

4.   #

5.   #

6.   #

7.   #

8.   #

MY CATCH OF THE DAY WAS

FISHING TRIP SCALE OF AWESOME

FISHING NOTE

FISHING DISCOVERIES

MY FISHING LOG

DATE :   (SUN MON TUE WED THU FRI SAT)

LOCATION :

FISHING WITH :

BAIT AND TOOL USED :

WEATHER :   TEMP :

START TIME :   END TIME :

TOTAL TIME USED :

TYPE OF FISH | NUMBER I CAUGHT

1. #
2. #
3. #
4. #
5. #
6. #
7. #
8. #

MY CATCH OF THE DAY WAS

FISHING TRIP SCALE OF AWESOME

FISHING NOTE

FISHING DISCOVERIES

MY FISHING LOG

DATE :   (SUN MON TUE WED THU FRI SAT)

LOCATION :

FISHING WITH :

BAIT AND TOOL USED :

WEATHER :   TEMP :

START TIME :   END TIME :

TOTAL TIME USED :

TYPE OF FISH | NUMBER I CAUGHT

1.   #

2.   #

3.   #

4.   #

5.   #

6.   #

7.   #

8.   #

MY CATCH OF THE DAY WAS

FISHING TRIP SCALE OF AWESOME

FISHING NOTE

FISHING DISCOVERIES

MY FISHING LOG

DATE :   (SUN MON TUE WED THU FRI SAT)

LOCATION :

FISHING WITH :

BAIT AND TOOL USED :

WEATHER :   TEMP :

START TIME :   END TIME :

TOTAL TIME USED :

TYPE OF FISH | NUMBER I CAUGHT

1.   #

2.   #

3.   #

4.   #

5.   #

6.   #

7.   #

8.   #

MY CATCH OF THE DAY WAS

FISHING TRIP SCALE OF AWESOME

FISHING NOTE

FISHING DISCOVERIES

MY FISHING LOG

DATE :   (SUN MON TUE WED THU FRI SAT)

LOCATION :

FISHING WITH :

BAIT AND TOOL USED :

WEATHER :   TEMP :

START TIME :   END TIME :

TOTAL TIME USED :

TYPE OF FISH | NUMBER I CAUGHT

1.   #

2.   #

3.   #

4.   #

5.   #

6.   #

7.   #

8.   #

MY CATCH OF THE DAY WAS

FISHING TRIP SCALE OF AWESOME

FISHING NOTE

FISHING DISCOVERIES

MY FISHING LOG

DATE :   (SUN MON TUE WED THU FRI SAT)

LOCATION :

FISHING WITH :

BAIT AND TOOL USED :

WEATHER :   TEMP :

START TIME :   END TIME :

TOTAL TIME USED :

TYPE OF FISH | NUMBER I CAUGHT

1.   #

2.   #

3.   #

4.   #

5.   #

6.   #

7.   #

8.   #

MY CATCH OF THE DAY WAS

FISHING TRIP SCALE OF AWESOME

☆ ☆ ☆ ☆ ☆

FISHING NOTE

FISHING DISCOVERIES

MY FISHING LOG

DATE :   (SUN MON TUE WED THU FRI SAT)

LOCATION :

FISHING WITH :

BAIT AND TOOL USED :

WEATHER :   TEMP :

START TIME :   END TIME :

TOTAL TIME USED :

TYPE OF FISH | NUMBER I CAUGHT

1. #
2. #
3. #
4. #
5. #
6. #
7. #
8. #

MY CATCH OF THE DAY WAS

FISHING TRIP SCALE OF AWESOME

FISHING NOTE

FISHING DISCOVERIES

MY FISHING LOG

DATE : (SUN MON TUE WED THU FRI SAT)

LOCATION :

FISHING WITH :

BAIT AND TOOL USED :

WEATHER :   TEMP :

START TIME :   END TIME :

TOTAL TIME USED :

TYPE OF FISH | NUMBER I CAUGHT

1. #
2. #
3. #
4. #
5. #
6. #
7. #
8. #

MY CATCH OF THE DAY WAS

FISHING TRIP SCALE OF AWESOME

FISHING NOTE

FISHING DISCOVERIES

MY FISHING LOG

DATE :   (SUN MON TUE WED THU FRI SAT)

LOCATION :

FISHING WITH :

BAIT AND TOOL USED :

WEATHER :   TEMP :

START TIME :   END TIME :

TOTAL TIME USED :

TYPE OF FISH | NUMBER I CAUGHT

1.   #
2.   #
3.   #
4.   #
5.   #
6.   #
7.   #
8.   #

MY CATCH OF THE DAY WAS

FISHING TRIP SCALE OF AWESOME

FISHING NOTE

FISHING DISCOVERIES

MY FISHING LOG

DATE :   (SUN MON TUE WED THU FRI SAT)

LOCATION :

FISHING WITH :

BAIT AND TOOL USED :

WEATHER :   TEMP :

START TIME :   END TIME :

TOTAL TIME USED :

TYPE OF FISH | NUMBER I CAUGHT

1. #

2. #

3. #

4. #

5. #

6. #

7. #

8. #

MY CATCH OF THE DAY WAS

FISHING TRIP SCALE OF AWESOME

FISHING NOTE

FISHING DISCOVERIES

MY FISHING LOG

DATE :   (SUN MON TUE WED THU FRI SAT)

LOCATION :

FISHING WITH :

BAIT AND TOOL USED :

WEATHER :   TEMP :

START TIME :   END TIME :

TOTAL TIME USED :

TYPE OF FISH | NUMBER I CAUGHT

1.   #
2.   #
3.   #
4.   #
5.   #
6.   #
7.   #
8.   #

MY CATCH OF THE DAY WAS

FISHING TRIP SCALE OF AWESOME

FISHING NOTE

FISHING DISCOVERIES

MY FISHING LOG

DATE :   (SUN MON TUE WED THU FRI SAT)

LOCATION :

FISHING WITH :

BAIT AND TOOL USED :

WEATHER :   TEMP :

START TIME :   END TIME :

TOTAL TIME USED :

TYPE OF FISH	NUMBER I CAUGHT
1.	#
2.	#
3.	#
4.	#
5.	#
6.	#
7.	#
8.	#

MY CATCH OF THE DAY WAS

FISHING TRIP SCALE OF AWESOME

FISHING NOTE

FISHING DISCOVERIES

MY FISHING LOG

DATE :   (SUN MON TUE WED THU FRI SAT)

LOCATION :

FISHING WITH :

BAIT AND TOOL USED :

WEATHER :   TEMP :

START TIME :   END TIME :

TOTAL TIME USED :

TYPE OF FISH | NUMBER I CAUGHT

1.   #

2.   #

3.   #

4.   #

5.   #

6.   #

7.   #

8.   #

MY CATCH OF THE DAY WAS

FISHING TRIP SCALE OF AWESOME

FISHING NOTE

FISHING DISCOVERIES

MY FISHING LOG

DATE :   (SUN MON TUE WED THU FRI SAT)

LOCATION :

FISHING WITH :

BAIT AND TOOL USED :

WEATHER :   TEMP :

START TIME :   END TIME :

TOTAL TIME USED :

TYPE OF FISH | NUMBER I CAUGHT

1.   #
2.   #
3.   #
4.   #
5.   #
6.   #
7.   #
8.   #

MY CATCH OF THE DAY WAS

FISHING TRIP SCALE OF AWESOME

FISHING NOTE

FISHING DISCOVERIES

MY FISHING LOG

DATE : (SUN MON TUE WED THU FRI SAT)

LOCATION :

FISHING WITH :

BAIT AND TOOL USED :

WEATHER :   TEMP :

START TIME :   END TIME :

TOTAL TIME USED :

TYPE OF FISH | NUMBER I CAUGHT

1. #
2. #
3. #
4. #
5. #
6. #
7. #
8. #

MY CATCH OF THE DAY WAS

FISHING TRIP SCALE OF AWESOME

FISHING NOTE

FISHING DISCOVERIES

MY FISHING LOG

DATE :   (SUN MON TUE WED THU FRI SAT)

LOCATION :

FISHING WITH :

BAIT AND TOOL USED :

WEATHER :   TEMP :

START TIME :   END TIME :

TOTAL TIME USED :

TYPE OF FISH | NUMBER I CAUGHT

1. #
2. #
3. #
4. #
5. #
6. #
7. #
8. #

MY CATCH OF THE DAY WAS

FISHING TRIP SCALE OF AWESOME

FISHING NOTE

FISHING DISCOVERIES

MY FISHING LOG

DATE :   (SUN MON TUE WED THU FRI SAT)
LOCATION :
FISHING WITH :
BAIT AND TOOL USED :

WEATHER :   TEMP :
START TIME :   END TIME :
TOTAL TIME USED :

TYPE OF FISH | NUMBER I CAUGHT

1.   #
2.   #
3.   #
4.   #
5.   #
6.   #
7.   #
8.   #

MY CATCH OF THE DAY WAS

FISHING TRIP SCALE OF AWESOME

FISHING NOTE

FISHING DISCOVERIES

MY FISHING LOG

DATE :   (SUN MON TUE WED THU FRI SAT)

LOCATION :

FISHING WITH :

BAIT AND TOOL USED :

WEATHER :   TEMP :

START TIME :   END TIME :

TOTAL TIME USED :

TYPE OF FISH | NUMBER I CAUGHT

1.   #

2.   #

3.   #

4.   #

5.   #

6.   #

7.   #

8.   #

MY CATCH OF THE DAY WAS

FISHING TRIP SCALE OF AWESOME

FISHING NOTE

FISHING DISCOVERIES

MY FISHING LOG

DATE :   (SUN MON TUE WED THU FRI SAT)

LOCATION :

FISHING WITH :

BAIT AND TOOL USED :

WEATHER :   TEMP :

START TIME :   END TIME :

TOTAL TIME USED :

TYPE OF FISH | NUMBER I CAUGHT

1.   #
2.   #
3.   #
4.   #
5.   #
6.   #
7.   #
8.   #

MY CATCH OF THE DAY WAS

FISHING TRIP SCALE OF AWESOME

FISHING NOTE

FISHING DISCOVERIES

MY FISHING LOG

DATE :   (SUN MON TUE WED THU FRI SAT)

LOCATION :

FISHING WITH :

BAIT AND TOOL USED :

WEATHER :   TEMP :

START TIME :   END TIME :

TOTAL TIME USED :

TYPE OF FISH | NUMBER I CAUGHT

1.   #
2.   #
3.   #
4.   #
5.   #
6.   #
7.   #
8.   #

MY CATCH OF THE DAY WAS

FISHING TRIP SCALE OF AWESOME

FISHING NOTE

FISHING DISCOVERIES

MY FISHING LOG

DATE : (SUN MON TUE WED THU FRI SAT)

LOCATION :

FISHING WITH :

BAIT AND TOOL USED :

WEATHER : TEMP :

START TIME : END TIME :

TOTAL TIME USED :

TYPE OF FISH | NUMBER I CAUGHT

1. #

2. #

3. #

4. #

5. #

6. #

7. #

8. #

MY CATCH OF THE DAY WAS

FISHING TRIP SCALE OF AWESOME

FISHING NOTE

FISHING DISCOVERIES

MY FISHING LOG

DATE :   (SUN MON TUE WED THU FRI SAT)

LOCATION :

FISHING WITH :

BAIT AND TOOL USED :

WEATHER :   TEMP :

START TIME :   END TIME :

TOTAL TIME USED :

TYPE OF FISH	NUMBER I CAUGHT
1.	#
2.	#
3.	#
4.	#
5.	#
6.	#
7.	#
8.	#

MY CATCH OF THE DAY WAS

FISHING TRIP SCALE OF AWESOME

FISHING NOTE

FISHING DISCOVERIES

MY FISHING LOG

DATE :   (SUN MON TUE WED THU FRI SAT)

LOCATION :

FISHING WITH :

BAIT AND TOOL USED :

WEATHER :   TEMP :

START TIME :   END TIME :

TOTAL TIME USED :

TYPE OF FISH | NUMBER I CAUGHT

1.   #
2.   #
3.   #
4.   #
5.   #
6.   #
7.   #
8.   #

MY CATCH OF THE DAY WAS

FISHING TRIP SCALE OF AWESOME

FISHING NOTE

FISHING DISCOVERIES

MY FISHING LOG

DATE :   (SUN MON TUE WED THU FRI SAT)

LOCATION :

FISHING WITH :

BAIT AND TOOL USED :

WEATHER :   TEMP :

START TIME :   END TIME :

TOTAL TIME USED :

TYPE OF FISH | NUMBER I CAUGHT

1.   #
2.   #
3.   #
4.   #
5.   #
6.   #
7.   #
8.   #

MY CATCH OF THE DAY WAS

FISHING TRIP SCALE OF AWESOME

FISHING NOTE

FISHING DISCOVERIES

MY FISHING LOG

DATE :   (SUN MON TUE WED THU FRI SAT)

LOCATION :

FISHING WITH :

BAIT AND TOOL USED :

WEATHER :   TEMP :

START TIME :   END TIME :

TOTAL TIME USED :

TYPE OF FISH | NUMBER I CAUGHT

1.   #
2.   #
3.   #
4.   #
5.   #
6.   #
7.   #
8.   #

MY CATCH OF THE DAY WAS

FISHING TRIP SCALE OF AWESOME

FISHING NOTE

FISHING DISCOVERIES

MY FISHING LOG

DATE :   (SUN MON TUE WED THU FRI SAT)

LOCATION :

FISHING WITH :

BAIT AND TOOL USED :

WEATHER :   TEMP :

START TIME :   END TIME :

TOTAL TIME USED :

TYPE OF FISH	NUMBER I CAUGHT
1.	#
2.	#
3.	#
4.	#
5.	#
6.	#
7.	#
8.	#

MY CATCH OF THE DAY WAS

FISHING TRIP SCALE OF AWESOME

FISHING NOTE

FISHING DISCOVERIES

MY FISHING LOG

DATE :   (SUN MON TUE WED THU FRI SAT)

LOCATION :

FISHING WITH :

BAIT AND TOOL USED :

WEATHER :   TEMP :

START TIME :   END TIME :

TOTAL TIME USED :

TYPE OF FISH | NUMBER I CAUGHT

1.   #

2.   #

3.   #

4.   #

5.   #

6.   #

7.   #

8.   #

MY CATCH OF THE DAY WAS

FISHING TRIP SCALE OF AWESOME

FISHING NOTE

FISHING DISCOVERIES

MY FISHING LOG

DATE :   (SUN MON TUE WED THU FRI SAT)

LOCATION :

FISHING WITH :

BAIT AND TOOL USED :

WEATHER :   TEMP :

START TIME :   END TIME :

TOTAL TIME USED :

TYPE OF FISH | NUMBER I CAUGHT

1.   #
2.   #
3.   #
4.   #
5.   #
6.   #
7.   #
8.   #

MY CATCH OF THE DAY WAS

FISHING TRIP SCALE OF AWESOME

FISHING NOTE

FISHING DISCOVERIES

MY FISHING LOG

DATE :   (SUN MON TUE WED THU FRI SAT)

LOCATION :

FISHING WITH :

BAIT AND TOOL USED :

WEATHER :   TEMP :

START TIME :   END TIME :

TOTAL TIME USED :

TYPE OF FISH | NUMBER I CAUGHT

1.   #
2.   #
3.   #
4.   #
5.   #
6.   #
7.   #
8.   #

MY CATCH OF THE DAY WAS

FISHING TRIP SCALE OF AWESOME

FISHING NOTE

FISHING DISCOVERIES

MY FISHING LOG

DATE :   (SUN MON TUE WED THU FRI SAT)

LOCATION :

FISHING WITH :

BAIT AND TOOL USED :

WEATHER :   TEMP :

START TIME :   END TIME :

TOTAL TIME USED :

TYPE OF FISH | NUMBER I CAUGHT

1.   #
2.   #
3.   #
4.   #
5.   #
6.   #
7.   #
8.   #

MY CATCH OF THE DAY WAS

FISHING TRIP SCALE OF AWESOME

FISHING NOTE

FISHING DISCOVERIES

MY FISHING LOG

DATE :   (SUN MON TUE WED THU FRI SAT)

LOCATION :

FISHING WITH :

BAIT AND TOOL USED :

WEATHER :   TEMP :

START TIME :   END TIME :

TOTAL TIME USED :

TYPE OF FISH	NUMBER I CAUGHT
1.	#
2.	#
3.	#
4.	#
5.	#
6.	#
7.	#
8.	#

MY CATCH OF THE DAY WAS

FISHING TRIP SCALE OF AWESOME

FISHING NOTE

FISHING DISCOVERIES

MY FISHING LOG

DATE :   (SUN MON TUE WED THU FRI SAT)

LOCATION :

FISHING WITH :

BAIT AND TOOL USED :

WEATHER :   TEMP :

START TIME :   END TIME :

TOTAL TIME USED :

TYPE OF FISH | NUMBER I CAUGHT

1.   #
2.   #
3.   #
4.   #
5.   #
6.   #
7.   #
8.   #

MY CATCH OF THE DAY WAS

FISHING TRIP SCALE OF AWESOME

FISHING NOTE

FISHING DISCOVERIES

MY FISHING LOG

DATE :   (SUN MON TUE WED THU FRI SAT)

LOCATION :

FISHING WITH :

BAIT AND TOOL USED :

WEATHER :   TEMP :

START TIME :   END TIME :

TOTAL TIME USED :

TYPE OF FISH | NUMBER I CAUGHT

1.   #
2.   #
3.   #
4.   #
5.   #
6.   #
7.   #
8.   #

MY CATCH OF THE DAY WAS

FISHING TRIP SCALE OF AWESOME

FISHING NOTE

FISHING DISCOVERIES

MY FISHING LOG

DATE :   (SUN MON TUE WED THU FRI SAT)

LOCATION :

FISHING WITH :

BAIT AND TOOL USED :

WEATHER :   TEMP :

START TIME :   END TIME :

TOTAL TIME USED :

TYPE OF FISH | NUMBER I CAUGHT

1.   #
2.   #
3.   #
4.   #
5.   #
6.   #
7.   #
8.   #

MY CATCH OF THE DAY WAS

FISHING TRIP SCALE OF AWESOME

FISHING NOTE

FISHING DISCOVERIES

MY FISHING LOG

DATE :   (SUN MON TUE WED THU FRI SAT)

LOCATION :

FISHING WITH :

BAIT AND TOOL USED :

WEATHER :   TEMP :

START TIME :   END TIME :

TOTAL TIME USED :

TYPE OF FISH | NUMBER I CAUGHT

1. #
2. #
3. #
4. #
5. #
6. #
7. #
8. #

MY CATCH OF THE DAY WAS

FISHING TRIP SCALE OF AWESOME

FISHING NOTE

FISHING DISCOVERIES

MY FISHING LOG

DATE :   (SUN MON TUE WED THU FRI SAT)

LOCATION :

FISHING WITH :

BAIT AND TOOL USED :

WEATHER :   TEMP :

START TIME :   END TIME :

TOTAL TIME USED :

TYPE OF FISH | NUMBER I CAUGHT

1.   #

2.   #

3.   #

4.   #

5.   #

6.   #

7.   #

8.   #

MY CATCH OF THE DAY WAS

FISHING TRIP SCALE OF AWESOME

FISHING NOTE

FISHING DISCOVERIES

Made in the USA
Monee, IL
07 July 2026

56551660R00057